SHIT GROUND
NO FANS

SHIT GROUND NO FANS

It's by far the greatest
FOOTBALL SONGBOOK
the world has ever seen...

J A C K   B R E M N E R

BANTAM PRESS

LONDON · TORONTO · SYDNEY · AUCKLAND · JOHANNESBURG

TRANSWORLD PUBLISHERS
61-63 Uxbridge Road, London W5 5SA
a division of The Random House Group Ltd

RANDOM HOUSE AUSTRALIA (PTY) LTD
20 Alfred Street, Milsons Point, Sydney,
New South Wales 2061, Australia

RANDOM HOUSE NEW ZEALAND LTD
18 Poland Road, Glenfield, Auckland 10, New Zealand

RANDOM HOUSE SOUTH AFRICA (PTY) LTD
Endulini, 5a Jubilee Road, Parktown 2193, South Africa

Published 2004 by Bantam Press, a division of Transworld Publishers

A catalogue record for this book is available from the British Library.
ISBN 0593 053761

Designed by www.carrstudio.co.uk
Printed at the Bath Press
1   3   5   7   9   10   8   6   4   2

Papers used by Transworld Publishers are natural, recyclable products made from
wood grown in sustainable forests. The manufacturing processes conform to the
environmental regulations of the country of origin.

Contents

Introduction

THE Poet Laureate Andrew Motion recently launched a competition to find his equivalent in the nation's football stadiums. Incredibly, he was offering a £10,000 prize to the winner, a man or woman upon whom he could bestow the name Chant Laureate (crap title, but for 10,000 quid he can call me anything he likes). Even more incredibly, only around 1,500 entries were received over the three months or so that the competition ran, in a country where over a million people regularly go to watch football every weekend. Surely this was worth a shot, I thought at the time of the launch, and, with pen in one hand, pint of snakebite and blackcurrant for inspiration in the other, I duly sat down to create the ultimate football chant. The judges were looking for the chants to have 'wit, inventiveness, energy and humour and the ability to be taken up by people on the terraces'. No problem.

Several hours later, knee-deep in screwed-up balls of paper and with clumps of my hair strewn across the table, my pint glass of snakebite shattered into a thousand pieces across the kitchen floor, I gave up and, cursing the name of Motion, retired to bed. It simply wasn't possible. You cannot just sit down and write a great football chant, I woke my wife to tell her. The whole point about football chants is that they are organic and spontaneous, born out of events unfolding at the time, on the pitch or off it. Like a good wisecrack, they come out of nowhere. Very interesting and good night, she said.

The lucky winner in the end was a Birmingham City fan who, weirdly, had penned a homage to Juan Pablo Angel, star striker of arch-rivals Aston Villa. I'm not bitter or anything and I'm sure that the bastard who won it will do the right thing and give all the money to an important charity, as the rest of us would have done. His winning chant was quite a clever little piece of street poetry, amusing in a very gentle, homely kind of way, and offensive to absolutely nobody. In short, it was the last chant you would ever hear at a British football ground. I will eat my grandma's woolly hat if, as the judges hoped, the chant is 'taken up by people on the terraces'. It just ain't gonna happen. Football fans don't do nice chants.

Traditional terrace humour is dark, unforgiving and vicious, aimed at hurting opposition fans, nasty policemen, big-nosed managers, perverted tight-fisted chairmen, fat players, illegitimate referees, their prostitute wives and mothers, drug-dealing, hubcap-thieving fathers

and, of course, the in-bred, miserably poor town they come from. It is humour based on ancient, deep-seated rivalries, a few degrees short of outright hatred. There are, of course, some innocent chants ('We love you, City, we do' etc) but they are very rarely funny. There are downright and fabulously silly ones too ('You only sing when you're fishing' to Grimsby fans, etc). There are also some brilliantly inventive

ones. I was sent one chant by a fan, which I have declined to include in this compilation for fear of upsetting either or both members of Britain's Christian community, who quite frankly will find more than enough to be upset about in this book as it is. (Forgive me, brothers and sisters.) This chant is almost Pythonesque. Allegedly sung over an Easter weekend to the traditional tune of 'You're going to get your f**king head kicked in', what he heard a group of fans singing was 'Jesus Christ will f**king rise again'. He didn't say where or when he heard it, and I have no idea whether it's true, but it neatly sums up the reality of football chants. It is irreverent, a bit shocking, slightly absurd, offensive to some people, but, and let's be honest here, it's very, very funny.

It doesn't necessarily follow that an obscene or offensive chant will be funny. Racist chants are offensive, but who, apart from a handful of cement-heads, finds them funny these days, or ever did, for that matter? Nor, necessarily, would Posh Spice exactly be rolling in the gangway on hearing some of the … er … um … how shall we put this? … the seaside-postcard-humour chants about her imaginary sex life with the whole of the Premier League and her alleged preference

for the tradesman's entrance over the front door, if you get my drift. (She should learn to see the funny side of things, that girl. No sense of humour at all.) But the dreadful truth is that the funniest football chants are often the cruellest and if I was Posh Spice I wouldn't go to another English football match in my life. I can hear it now as the hot tears stream down my cheeks: 'Bremner is a slapper/He's got no f**king tits …' (I have actually but that's another story.)

While compiling this book, I had one main criterion – the chant had to be funny. Some, frankly, were just way too obscene, offensive and libellous and even Bernard Manning or Roy Chubby Brown would probably blanch at the prospect of singing them. They were just too extreme, and the humour was lost as a result. Not long after the death of his son in a car crash with Princess Diana, Fulham owner Mohamed Al-Fayed had to endure the sound of some visiting Manchester City fans singing, 'Where's your Dodi gone?' That is a good example of a chant that oversteps the line. I have left all those ones out.

In a way that I have never had with jokes and gags, I have always had an ear for a good chant and have kept an informal collection of them down the years. So too, it seems, does everybody else who takes an interest in British football and it took only a few dozen emails and phone calls to open the floodgates of contributions. There are around 300 chants in this compilation, but I'm sure we have only scratched the surface. Every week somewhere in Britain, inside a stadium or on the way to it or in the pub beforehand, new and funny chants are being created and sung. Often they only live for a few weeks before losing their currency and are replaced by a new favourite or one-off. There must be thousands of them out there somewhere.

It is difficult to know where to begin thanking people for their contributions to this book. Little persuasion, however, was needed in parting contributors from their favourite funny football chants and I suppose I shouldn't have been amazed by the haste with which people were prepared to abandon whatever they were meant to be doing at work and start racking their brains and contacting their mates. The hunt for funny chants led me down some very interesting paths of inquiry, not least the one that, via about six strangers, led me to Tim Marshall, the Foreign Editor of Sky News and ardent Leeds fan, who, bless his little microphone and map of Iraq, could not have been more helpful had he been spelling out the likely route of Allied invasion through Kurdish-held territory in the north of the country. He's still sending me chants as I write. (That's enough now, Tim. There's a war on, for heaven's sake.) I also contacted fanzine editors at every club, venerable keepers of club humour and culture that they are, and to them I am hugely indebted too. Apart, that is, from the few crack-peddling rent-boys among them who didn't even have the common decency to reply. To you I say, may Howard Wilkinson become manager of your club. Those deserving of special thanks – and forgive me if I have missed anyone out – have contributed beyond the call of duty. They include Matt Johnstone (Motherwell), Jamie Stripe (Orient), Chris Spink (Portsmouth), Ben Richie (Southampton), David Pay (Plymouth), Paul Williams and the dozens of fellow Bournemouth fans he contacted, Martin Haythorne (Doncaster), Steve Wilson (Celtic and Wycombe), Ian Farrow at Hull City, Robert Nichols (Middlesbrough), Mike Raynsford (Crystal Palace), Stefano Blin (Chelsea), Henry Hainault (Arsenal) and Brian Gyng (Newcastle).

Thanks too to Doug Young, the editor at Transworld, for all his sound advice, and to his sales team for quite rightly binning my title for the book (*The Referee's Got BSE*) and suggesting the far more elegant and sophisticated title *Shit Ground No Fans*.

If you would like to contribute a song from the terraces to future editions, please send it in to mail@shitgroundnofans.co.uk

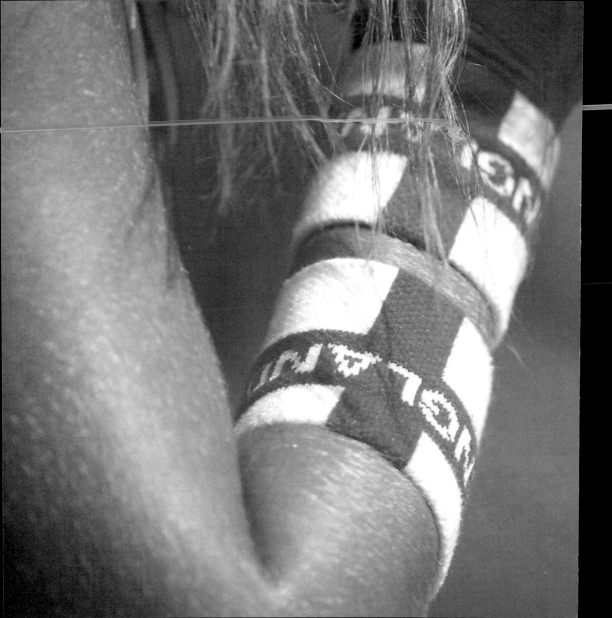

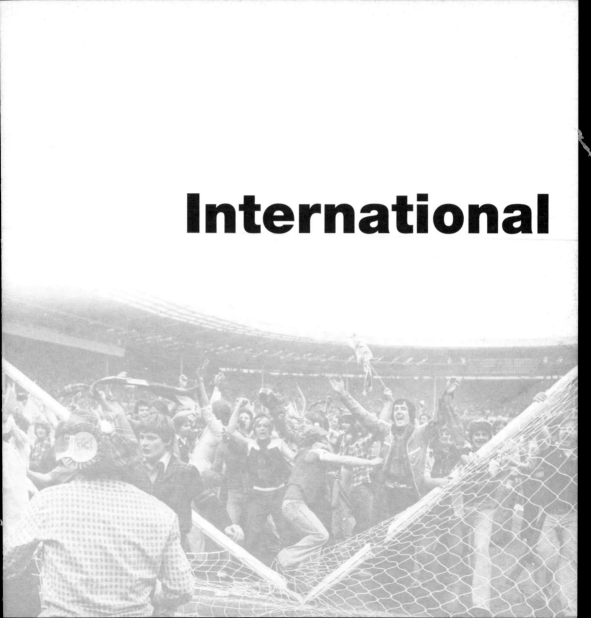

International

Deutschland
England

Olympiastadion
München

1 : 5

England

Michael Owen's magic

He wears a magic hat

And when he plays for England

He's a jolly decent chap

He scores them with his left

He scores them with his right

And when we play the Germans

He scores all f**king night

To the tune of 'My Old Man's A Dustman'. An old favourite adapted to celebrate Owen's hat-trick in the 5–1 demolition of Rudi Voeller's Germany in Munich on 1 September 2001.

One–nil down

Five–one up

Two World Wars and one World Cup

With a nick nack paddy whack

Give a dog a bone

Rudi Voeller f**ked off home

Cheer up, Craigie Brown

Oh what can I say

To a sad Scottish bastard

And a shite football team

To the tune of 'Daydream Believer'.

You're just the shit part of England

The shit part of England (*ad infinitum*)

To the tune of 'Guantanamera'; sung to Scots, Welsh, Northern Irish.

Oh David Beckham
He wears a magic hat
He went to Japan and said I fancy that
He wouldn't play for Scotland
Or Wales cos they're shite
He said I'll play for Ing-er-lund
Cos they're fucking dynamite.

To the tune of 'My Old Man's A Dustman'.

If it wasn't for the English you'd be Krauts (x2)
If it wasn't for the English
Wasn't for the English
If it wasn't for the English you'd be Krauts

To the tune of 'She'll Be Coming Round The Mountain'. Sung to the fans of any country that was occupied by the forces of Nazi Germany, but belted out with special feeling against the French, Belgians and Dutch.

Maradona is a wanker
He wears a wanker's hat
He's retired and fat now
But he's still a f**king twat
He f**ked up on the left wing
He f**ked up on the right
He had to cheat England
Cos the Argies are total shite

To the tune of 'My Old Man's A Dustman'.

You can stick your f**king Euro up your arse (x2)
You can stick your f**king Euro
Stick your f**king Euro
You can stick your f**king Euro up your arse

To the tune of 'She'll Be Coming Round The Mountain'. Sung to anyone from the Eurozone silly enough to abandon their traditional currency.

Are you Scotland (x2)

Are you Scotland in disguise? (x2)

To the tune of 'Bread Of Heaven'. Sung to teams losing or playing poorly.

You'll never take the Falklands

Tune: none. Repeat until a new war breaks out.

Scotland

We stole your goalposts
Your lovely goalposts
We stole your goalposts
And your Wembley pitch too
You never knew how much you'd miss them
Till we took your goalposts away

To the tune of 'You Are My Sunshine', Scotland fans take a trip down memory lane to recall the day in 1977 when around 10,000 of their fathers stormed the pitch at Wembley for an unscheduled Bay City Roller look-alike competition.

You put your left hand in
Your left hand out
In out in out
Then shake it all about
You do the Maradona and you turn around
He put the English out!

Oh Diego Maradona
Oh Diego Maradona
Oh Diego Maradona
He put the English out out out!

You put your right foot in
Your right foot out
In out in out
Then shake it all about
You do the Chrissy Waddle and you turn around
He put the English out!

Oh Chrissy Chrissy Waddle
Oh Chrissy Chrissy Waddle
Oh Chrissy Chrissy Waddle
He put the English out out out!

You put your left foot in
Your left foot out
In out in out
Then shake it all about
You do the Tommy Brolin and you turn around
He put the English out!

Oh Tommy Tommy Brolin
Oh Tommy Tommy Brolin
Oh Tommy Tommy Brolin
He put the English out out out!

To the tune of 'Hokey Cokey'. Hailing Argentina's Maradona (Mexico 1986), the missed penalty of Englishman Chris Waddle (Italia 90) and the chubby Swede Thomas Brolin (Euro 92). All of them heroes in Scottish football's Hall of Fame.

S-C-O-T-S
We are S-C-O-T-S
We are S, super Scotland
We are C, completely barmy
We are O, on the bevvy
We are T, Tartan army
Singing ... we are S-C-O-T-S

Tune: 'D-I-S-C-O'.

They're going home, they're going home
England's going home
Three lions on your shirt, two goals past Seaman
Fifteen pints last night, Gascoigne's f**king
    steaming
They're going home, they're going home
England's going home

To the tune of 'Three Lions'. Sympathy from Scotland fans after England's
semi-final defeat against Germany at Euro 96.

Who put the ball in the England net?
Arfur, Arfur
Who put the ball in the England net?
Arfur, Arfur f**king Europe

Who put the ball in the England net?
Olaf, Olaf
Who put the ball in the England net?
Olaf, Olaf f**king Europe

This second verse only works if you have a) the thickest of Scottish accents or b) a throat full of crushed rough oatcakes.

One team in Tallin
There's only one team in Tallin
There's only one team in Tallin

To the tune of 'Guantanamera'. Scotland fans try to see the funny side after the Estonia team failed to appear on the pitch for a World Cup qualifier, in a dispute over rescheduled kick-off time.

Wem-ber-lee, Wem-ber-lee
Was the finest pitch in Europe till we took it all away

Sing when you're whaling
You only sing when you're whaling (*ad infinitum*)

To the tune of 'Guantanamera', sung in matches against Norway and the Faroe Islands.

Save the whales
Save the whales
We're the famous Tartan Army
And we're here to save the whales

To the tune of 'Wem-ber-lee! Wem-ber-lee!'

Wales

You can shove your Royal Family up your arse (x2)
You can shove your Royal Family
Shove your Royal Family
You can shove your Royal Family up your arse

You can stick your f**king chariots up your arse (x2)
You can stick your f**king chariots
Stick your f**king chariots
You can stick your f**king chariots up your arse

You can stick your David Beckham up your arse (x2)
You can stick your David Beckham
Stick your David Beckham
You can stick your David Beckham up your arse

To the tune of 'She'll Be Coming Round The Mountain'.

Dance, dance, wherever you may be
We've got a star called Craig Bellamy
He beats defenders and leaves them on their arse
A football genius on the park
He danced around the Danes and got us a win
He danced around the Argies and fired one in
He danced around Veron and Cannigia
Because they're shite
And he plays for the boys in red and white

To the tune of 'Lord Of The Dance'.

Mae hen wlad fy nhadau yn annwyl i mi
Gwlad beirdd a chantorion, enwogion o fri
Ei gwrol ryfelwyr gwladgarwyr tra mad
Dros ryddid collasant eu gwaed

Gwlad! gwlad! pleidiol wyf i'm gwlad
Tra môr yn fur
I'r bur hoff bau
O bydded i'r heniaith barhau

Hen Gymru fynyddig, paradwys y bardd
Ob dyffryn, pob clogwyn, i'm golwg sydd hardd
Trwy deimlad gwladgarol mor swynol yw si
Ei nentydd, afonydd i mi

Os treisiodd y gelyn fy ngwlad dan ei droed
Mae heniaith y Cymry mor fyw ag erioed
Ni luddiwyd yr awen gan erchyll law brad
Ni thelyn berseiniol fy ngwlad

Tune: 'Land Of My Fathers', the Welsh national anthem. Not a lot you can say to that …

Clubs A–Z

Aberdeen

The wrong f**king country
You're in the wrong f**king country

Sung to Rangers and Celtic fans to the tune of 'Guantanamera'.

We're red, you're dead
We're bouncing on your head
Aberdeen, Aberdeen

Tune: traditional.

No soap in Glasgow
There's no soap in Glasgow (x10)

To the tune of 'Guantanamera'

Northern Ireland is shit (x10)

Also sung to Rangers and Celtic fans to traditional 'We Love You, We Do' tune.

Arsenal

Osama, whoa-oa-oa

Osama, whoa-oa-oa

He supports the Ar-se-nal

He's hiding near Kabul

To the tune of 'Volare', after newspaper reports that as a young man Bin Laden supported Arsenal.

Drink, drink wherever you may be

We are the drunk and disorderly

And we don't give a shit and we don't give a f**k

Cos we came home with the Cup Winners' Cup

To the tune of 'Lord Of The Dance', sung following surprise win over Parma in Copenhagen 1994.

Cole!

Always believe in your soul

You've got the power to know

That you're indestructible

Always believe in

Ashley Cole, Cole!

To the tune of 'Gold', by Spandau Ballet. Also sung for Joe Cole at West Ham as well as any other player up and down the country whose name rhymes with 'soul'.

He's blond, he's quick

His name's a porno flick

Emmanuel, Emmanuel

Tribute to the golden-maned French midfielder Emmanuel Petit, to the traditional tune of 'Wem-ber-lee! Wem-ber-lee!'

Vieira, woo-aooo
Vieira, woo-aooo
He comes from Sen-e-gal
He plays for the Ars-e-nal

To the tune of 'Volare'.

One British Airways
There's only one British Airways

Sung to the tune of 'Guantanamera' and aimed at Arsenal's Dennis Bergkamp, who has a deep fear of flying. The singers often hold their arms out to the side in the manner of an aeroplane just in case Dennis can't hear. You may have seen them on television when the Dutchman goes to take a corner at an away ground.

Home in five minutes
You'll all be home in five minutes
Home in five minutes

Taunting visiting Man United fans to the tune of 'Guantanamera'.

Aston Villa

Roll along, Aston Villa, roll along
To the top of the League where you belong
There'll be cups and trophies too
For the boys in claret and blue
Roll along, Aston Villa, roll along

Roll along, shitty City, roll along
To the bottom of the League where you belong
There'll be cups and saucers too
For the boys in royal blue
Roll along, shitty City, roll along

Sung to the tune of 'She'll Be Coming Round The Mountain'.

Birmingham, are you listening?

To the song we are singing?

We're walking along

Singing our song

Shitting on the City as we go

Sung to the tune of 'Walking In A Winter Wonderland'.

Barnsley

Bra-zil
It's just like watching Bra-zil

To the tune of 'Blue Moon', sung with no little irony following the Yorkshire club's promotion to the top flight.

D-I-WAN-KEY-O
D-I-WAN-KEY-O
D-I-WAN-KEY-O

Sung for Paolo Di Canio to the tune of 1970s classic 'D-I-S-C-O'.

Birmingham City

Don't cry for me, Aston Villa
The truth is I cannot stand you
All through my wild days
My mad existence
We took the Holte End
Without resistance

To the tune of 'Don't Cry For Me, Argentina'.

We are Brummies, we are Brummies
We are Brummies, yes we are
You are wankers, you are wankers
You are wankers, yes you are

To the tune of 'Sailing'.

Sing when you're robbing

You only sing when you're robbing

To the tune of 'Guantanamera'. A traditional Birmingham welcome for Liverpool and Everton fans, often followed in recent years by:

He-e-e-ey Scousers

Ooh! Ah!

I want to kno-o-o-ow

Where's my vide-o?

To the tune of 'Hey Baby!'

You can stick your Jasper Carrott up your arse (x2)

You can stick your Jasper Carrott

Stick your Jasper Carrott

Stick your Jasper Carrott up your arse

Has been sung by opposition fans to the tune of 'She'll Be Coming Round The Mountain' when the great Midlands comedian is spotted among the Birmingham faithful.

Blackburn Rovers

Damian Duff, Damian Duff

Running down the wing

Damian Duff, Damian Duff

Running down the wing

Gets the f**king ball

Scores a f**king goal

Damian Duff, Damian Duff, Damian Duff!

Sung to the tune of 'Robin Hood, Riding Through The Glen' – until the Irishman slipped off to Chelsea to take the Russian rouble …

Start spreading the news
He's playing today
I want to see him score again
Dwight Yorke, Dwight Yorke
If he can score from there
He'll score from anywhere
It's up to you
Dwight Yorke, Dwight Yorke

Sung to the tune of 'New York, New York'; also by Villa and Man United
fans during his spells there.

Blackpool

Away in a manger

No crib for a bed

The little Lord Jesus looked up and he said:

F**k off, Preston!

F**k off, Preston!

Burnley have also been known to receive a rendition of this Christmas favourite.

Come on a donkey

You must have come on a donkey

Blackpool fans are often treated to this one when only a few have been able to make it to an away ground.

Bolton Wanderers

Andy Cole, Andy Cole

He gets the ball

He does f**k all

Andy, Andy Cole

A warm reception, to the tune of 'Hi! Ho!' for the Blackburn Rovers and former Man United forward.

We've got chickens in our backyard

We feed them on Indian corn

But one's a bugger

For giving the other

A piggyback over the wall

The origins and point of this quirky one have never been fully established.

O-K-O

C-H-A

You've got no one like Jay Jay

With a nick nack paddy whack

Give a dog a bone

Why don't Rovers f**k off home!

One of many hymns to the fans' favourite Jay Jay Okocha, and a slap to rivals Blackburn while they are about it.

Boston United

We're cheats and we know we are

We're cheats and we know we are

Pilgrims fans take ironic delight in their club being fined and docked points for financial irregularities at the end of the 2001/02 season.

You fill up my senses

Like a gallon of Batemans

Like a packet of Seasalt

Like a good pickled egg

Like a night out in Boston

Like a greasy chip buttie

Like Boston United

Come fill me again!

Boston's fans are not the first or only ones to sing this or a variation – to the tune of 'Annie's Song' – but it is bit of a favourite at this otherwise chorally challenged club.

Bournemouth

We all love our grannies and our grandads too
We all love our grannies, come on, don't you?
All together now

The south coast club are not blessed with the biggest or most original songbook in the football league, but this one, to the tune of 'Over Land And Sea', pays moving respect to the town's retirement community.

The following is either desperately sad or superbly ironic – a boast to other teams from coastal towns, generally Blackpool, that their beach has been awarded a European blue flag for cleanliness …

We've got a blue flag

We've got a blue flag

You ain't!

You ain't!

What's it like to (x2)

What's it like to see the sun?

Sung to Wigan fans to the tune of 'Bread Of Heaven'.

Bradford City

They think their ground's fantastic
But it's just made of plastic
Andy Booth's a _____
The Hudders family

A politically incorrect snipe at Yorkshire neighbours Huddersfield, their state-of-the-art stadium and former top striker. And if that doesn't get a rise, then ...

Their sisters are their mothers
Their fathers are their brothers
They like to f**k each other
They're the Hudders family

Brentford

Build a bonfire, build a bonfire

Put the Fulham on the top

Queens Park Rangers in the middle

And let's torch the f**king lot

A terrace classic, sung to the tune of 'Oh My Darling Clementine' and adapted for the purposes of this West London rivalry.

Vauxhall! Vauxhall Motors!

They're the greatest team in history

From a small pub! In Ellesmere!

They knocked Rangers

Out on pen-al-ties

Sung to the *Flintstones* theme tune, this one celebrates Brentford's delight following the FA Cup defeat of QPR by the car workers of Vauxhall in 2002.

Brighton & Hove Albion

Two Kerry Mayos
There's only two Kerry Mayos

A witty take on the traditional 'There's Only One …'
The Brighton left-back, weirdly, has a wife with the same Christian name.

In a town where I was born
There lived a man
Who sailed the seas
He was big and he was Dutch
And he doesn't let in much
Michael Kuipers is a former Dutch marine,
a former Dutch marine, a former Dutch marine (x2)

A Beatles tribute to the Brighton goalkeeper.

Brighton fans have long had to endure the somewhat dated and politically incorrect jibes of rival fans about the city's large gay community. Here are some of the more printable taunts:

You're going down with your boyfriend ...

Does your boyfriend (x2)
Does your boyfriend know you're here? (x2)

We can see you (x2)
We can see you holding hands (x2)

Both sung to the tune of 'Bread Of Heaven'.

On a more wholesome and innocent note, opposition fans have also taken issue with Brighton fans over their seasonal employment patterns and the collapse of one of their famous piers ...

You only work in the summer
Work in the summer
You only work in the summer

Sung to the tune of 'Guantanamera'.

Down with the pier

You're going down with the pier (*repeat till bored*)

I know a fat old policeman

He's always on the beat

That fat and jolly red-faced man

He really is a treat

You'll always find him laughing

He's never known to frown

The reason for his jollity

Is that Brighton's going down

Only known to be sung by Crystal Palace fans, who have a special contempt for Brighton. Don't ask …

Bristol City

City, wherever you may be
We went down from One to Three
We'll be back through to win all three
We'll go down in history

To the tune of 'Lord Of The Dance'; one that makes Rovers fans laugh the loudest.

They should have built a wall not a bridge (x2)
They should have built a wall
Should have a built a wall
They should have built a wall not a bridge

Sung to Cardiff and Swansea fans to the tune of 'She'll Be Coming Round The Mountain', with a second verse for afters:

You can stick your f**king dragon up your arse (x2)
You can stick your f**king dragon
Stick your f**king dragon
You can stick your f**king dragon up your arse

Bristol Rovers

Always shit on the Welsh side of the bridge

La la la la la la la la

'Always Look On The Bright Side Of Life' – a favourite of both Bristol teams when they find themselves in the company of their friends from across the Severn.

If I had the wings of a sparrow

If I had the arse of a crow

I'd fly over City tomorrow

And shit on the bastards below

Shit on, shit on, shit on the bastards below below

Shit on, shit on, I'd shit on the bastards below

An old classic for neighbours the Robins, to the tune of 'My Bonnie Lies Over The Ocean'.

He's only a poor little Robin

His wings are all tattered and torn

He made me feel sick

So I hit him with a brick

And now he don't sing any more

To the tune of 'He's Only A Poor Little Sparrow'.

Burnley

You can shove your f**king tower up your arse (x2)

You can shove your f**king tower

Shove your f**king tower

You can shove your f**king tower up your arse

Sung to Blackpool fans to the tune of 'She'll Be Coming Round The Mountain'.

He's sewing bags
He's sewing bags
Oyston's sewing bags

To the tune of 'Three Lions',
a heartfelt tribute to the former
Blackpool chairman Oyston
after he was jailed for raping
a 16-year-old model.

Chairman Jackie Walker went up to the pearly
   gates (x3)
And this is what St Peter said:
Who the f**k are Bastard Rovers? (x3)
The Clarets go marching On! On! On!

To the tune of 'Mine Eyes Have Seen The Glory' – one for the former
chairman of bitter rivals Blackburn.

I went to an alehouse I often frequent
I saw Graeme Souness and all his money was spent
He asked me to play, I answered him Nay!
Saying rubbish like yours I can beat any day

And it's no, nay, never
No nay never no more
Till we play Blackburn Rovers
No never no more

Ewood Park is now empty, it's getting knocked down
Blackburn Rovers play their games on a strip of
   waste ground
Graeme Souness is on the touchline, says
   something's not right
There's far more players than supporters in sight

And it's no, nay, never
No nay never no more
Till we play Blackburn Rovers
No never no more

And now five years have passed and Burnley reign
   supreme
The League and the Cup will be won by our team
Blackburn Rovers are bankrupt and they've long
   since died
And now Graeme Souness sweeps Burnley's Long
   Side

Former Rovers manager Kenny Dalglish was also the subject of this
Burnley rendition of 'The Wild Rover'. But it is often met with the retort:

Your father had your mother
Your sister and your brother
You all sleep with one another
You're the Burnley family

Your town is twinned with Hell
You're ugly and you smell
This ought to ring a bell
You're the Burnley family

Bury

Shit fans, no songs.

Cambridge United

Cambridge are surprisingly uncreative for a town full of eggheads and boffins. Unsure quite how to taunt their hosts, some visiting fans have resorted to this version of 'She'll Be Coming Round The Mountain'. In the interests of fairness and equality, it has been heard in Oxford too …

You can shove your f**king boat race up your arse (x2)
You can shove your f**king boat race
Shove your f**king boat race
You can shove your f**king boat race up your arse

Cardiff City

Always shit on the English side of the bridge

To the tune of 'Always Look On The Bright Side Of Life'.

Cardiff fans often like to remind their West Country friends of their agricultural heritage and try to sing the following in a Wurzel-style accent:

I can't read

And I can't write

But that don't really matter

Cos I is a Bristol City (or Rovers) fan

And I can drive my tractor

Steer to the left

Steer to the right

It don't really matter

Cos when it comes to shagging my wife

I'd rather 'ave me tractor

Also …

You're going home on a combine harvester …

You can stick your f**king rugby up your arse (x2)
You can stick your f**king rugby
Stick your f**king rugby
You can stick your f**king rugby up your arse

To the tune of 'She'll Be Coming Round The Mountain' – one for their oval-shaped brothers at the Millennium Stadium and the Arms Park.

One–nil to the sheep-shaggers …

To the tune of 'Go West' after scoring the opening goal and often in response to:

You like shagging sheep
You like shagging sheep
You like shagging
You like shagging

You like shagging sheep

Sung to the tune of 'Knees Up Mother Brown'.

And:

I'd rather shag a woman than a sheep (x2)
I'd rather shag a woman
Rather shag a woman
Rather shag a woman than a sheep – sideways!

Sung to the tune of 'She'll Be Coming Round The Mountain'.

And …

What's it like to (x2)
What's it like to ram a lamb? (x2)

Another one sure to wind up the Cardiff faithful is …

You wish you were Ing-er-lish
You wish you were Ing-er-lish

Carlisle United

We'd rather shag a sheep than a lass (x2)
We'd rather shag a sheep
Rather shag a sheep
We'd rather shag a sheep than a lass

Bristolians are not the only fans with sheep issues, it seems.

Cumbria, my Lord, Cumbria
Cumbria, my Lord, Cumbria
Cumbria, my Lord, Cumbria
O Lord, Cumbria

To the tune of 'Kumbaya'.

Sung at Carlisle fans to the tune of 'Guantanamera':
A small town in Scotland
You're just a small town in Scotland

Celtic

Well I hope it's multi-storey when you jump (x2)
Hope it's multi-storey (x2)
Well I hope it's multi-storey when you jump

Well I hope it's spiky railings when you land (x2)
Hope it's spiky railings (x2)
Well I hope it's spiky railings when you land

Well I hope it's Catholic doctors when you die (x2)
Hope it's Catholic doctors (x2)
Well I hope it's Catholic doctors when you die

One of those lovely sectarian ones only Glasgow can produce, to the tune of 'She'll Be Coming Round The Mountain'.

You look through the dustbin for something to eat
You find a dead lobster and think it's a treat
In your Monaco slums!

An ironic take on the traditional 'Dead Rat' song, sung in Monaco during a Champions League match.

You are my Larsson, my Henrik Larsson
You make me happy when skies are grey
We went for Shearer
But he's a wanker
Please don't take my Larsson away

To the tune of 'You Are My Sunshine'.

Hey baby
Ooh ah
I want to know-ow-ow-ow
Who the fuck is Flo?

A warm welcome to Scotland for Rangers' signing Tore Andre Flo.

Charlton Athletic

Paolo was wandering across the pitch
Paolo, Paolo
Paolo was wandering across the pitch
Paolo, Paolo
Paolo was wandering across the pitch
Charlton are up, West Ham are down
We all know there's going to be a goal

To the tune of 'When Johnny Comes Marching Home'. Charlton fans taunt their London rivals following the transfer of Italian striker Paolo Di Canio. And while we're about it, why not have a pop at former Addicks favourite Defoe, who went the other way a few years earlier:

F**k off, Jermaine Defoe
We've got Di Canio
F**k off, Jermaine Defoe
We've got Di Canio

To the tune of Verdi's 'La Donna E Mobile'. Marginally more sophisticated than …

Let's all laugh at Palace
Let's all laugh at Palace

The same tune as 'Let's All Have A Disco/Let's All Do The Conga/Let's Go F**king Mental' etc …

Rufus is a dog's name (x2)
La la la la

Tottenham fans taunt Charlton Athletic defender Richard Rufus.

Chelsea

Debt-free wherever you may be
We're going to buy everyone we see
And we don't give a f**k
About the transfer fee
Cos we are the wealthy CFC

To the tune of 'Lord Of The Dance'. A witty adaptation of the traditional 'Carefree …' and inspired by the arrival of billionaire owner Roman Abramovich.

Sing when it's snowing
You only sing when it's snowing

To the tune of 'Guantanamera'. To fans of Norwegian club Tromso during a blizzard-hit European Cup game in the Arctic Circle. In the return leg, Chelsea fans continued the joke with:

What's it like to (x2)
What's it like to play on grass? (x2)

To the tune of 'Bread Of Heaven'.

You're French and you know you are
You're French and you know you are

To the tune of 'Go West', sung to FC Bruges fans in European game.

Is that all (x2)
Is that all she gets at home? (x2)

'Bread Of Heaven' tune sung by the Chelsea fans after the appearance of a male streaker.

You're shish and you know you are
You're shish and you know you are

Chelsea to the fans of Turkish club Galatasaray at Stamford Bridge.

He's here, he's there
We're not allowed to swear
Frank LeBoeuf! Frank LeBoeuf!

After the French defender said in the Chelsea programme that he did not like children to hear the more traditional:

He's here, he's there
He's every-f**king-where
Frank LeBoeuf! Frank LeBoeuf!

Blue is the colour, football is the game
Poor old Matthew Harding
Should've caught the train

This darkly comic parody of Chelsea's 'Blue Is The Colour' was sung by some of their rivals' less sensitive fans following the death of director Matthew Harding in a helicopter crash.

Cheltenham Town

They go down the cellar for something to eat
They find a dead body and think it's a treat
In their Gloucester slums!

Perhaps the only football song inspired by a serial killer, Fred West, a native of Gloucester.

Chesterfield

You can shove your crooked spire up your arse (x2)
You can shove your crooked spire
Shove your crooked spire
You can shove your crooked spire up your arse

To the tune of 'She'll Be Coming Round The Mountain'. Chesterfield fans, it seems, have precious few original words with which to respond to this mocking of their famous spire.

Colchester United

Shit fans, no songs.

Coventry City

Oh I do like to be beside the seaside
Oh I do like to be beside the sea
Oh I do like to walk along the prom, prom, prom
Where the brass bands play
F**k off West Brom and Birmingham
F**k off West Brom and Birmingham

We speak with an accent exceedingly rare
You want a cathedral we've got one to spare
In our Coventry homes
In our Coventry homes

To the tune of 'My Liverpool Home'.

Crewe Alexandra

Shit, shit, shit on the Lou (x3)
Shit on the Lou Macari!

Like most original Crewe songs, this one was inspired by a deep-seated hatred for anything to do with the 'Clayheads' from the Potteries, Stoke 'Joke' City or Port Vale. This one was sung for the benefit of the former Stoke City boss.

Crystal Palace

Away in a manger
No crib for a bed
The little Lord Jesus sat up and he said
We hate Millwall and we hate Millwall
We are the Millwall haters!

A little beauty for the former manager, who will be better remembered than a certain Steve Bruce, who left in acrimonious circumstances for the bright lights of Birmingham City:

Brucie the elephant packed his bag
And said goodbye to the Palace
Off he went like a greedy fat lump
C**t, c**t, c**t

Brucie the Elephant packed his cash
And trumbled off to the porn shop
Off he went to the Birmingham dump
C**t, c**t, c**t

I'd rather be Bin Laden than Steve Bruce (x2)

I'd rather be Bin Laden

Rather be Bin Laden

I'd rather be Bin Laden than Steve Bruce

To the tune of 'She'll Be Coming Round The Mountain'.

We scored five

They scored none

Brighton take it up the bum

With a nick nack paddy whack

Give a dog a bone

Why don't Brighton f**k off home

All in all you're just a bunch of pricks from Millwall!

To the tune of 'Brick In The Wall' by Pink Floyd, one for Palace's friends up the south London road.

There's only one Ian Dowie

One Ian Dowie

He's ugly as f**k

But he'll take us up

Walking in a Dowie wonderland

Just one Lombardo

Give him to me

He's from Juventus

In Italy

To the tune of 'O Sole Mio', a tribute to Italian striker 'Bald Eagle' Attilo Lombardo.

Darlington

The football league is upside down (x2)
We're going up with Carlisle
And Hartlepool are going down

To the tune of 'When The Saints Go Marching In'.

We hate Poolie, monkey-hangers
We hate Poolie, Poolie scum

To the tune of 'Sailing' – an historical reference to a curious incident in the Napoleonic Wars when the good people of Hartlepool hanged a monkey – washed ashore from a French wreck wearing full naval uniform – on spying charges.

Where's your monkey gone? (x4)

To the tune of 'Where's Your Mama Gone?'

Derby County

He's old and he shits himself (*ad infinitum*)

A tribute to their old Notts Forest friend, Des Walker.

There's only one Dessie Walker
Only one Dessie Walker
With his pension book and his zimmerframe
Dessie Walker's pissed himself again

To the tune of 'Winter Wonderland'. Derby fans remind the former England defender he's getting a little long in the tooth.

He's fat
He's round
He's taking Forest down
Joe Kinnear! Joe Kinnear!

A warm welcome following the arrival of the former Wimbledon boss at Notts Forest.

**Sing when you're shearing
You only sing when you're shearing!**

A response from the visitors, to the tune of 'Guantanamera'.

Doncaster Rovers

The following three chants were sung to former Liverpool and Denmark midfielder Jan Molby when he visited Belle Vue as manager of Kidderminster and was sent from the bench by the referee after losing his rag. You'll get the gist …

You've never seen a salad! (x10)

Have you ever, have you ever
Have you ever seen your feet? (x2)

To the tune of 'Bread Of Heaven'

Slimfast no chance, Slimfast no chance

To the tune of 'Big Ben Chimes'.

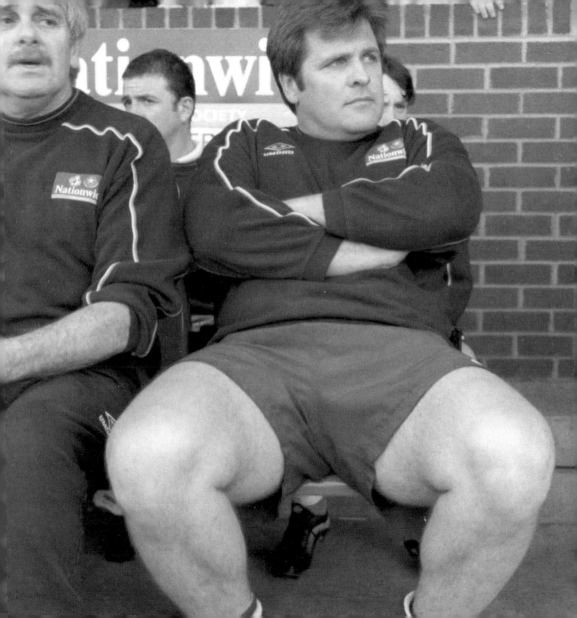

Dundee

You are a weegie

A smelly weegie

You're only happy on Giro day

Your mum's out stealing

Your dad's a dealer

Please don't take my hubcaps away

Tune: 'You Are My Sunshine'. (In case any English are wondering, a 'weegie' is a GlasWEGian.) Allegedly impoverished visitors from Glasgow are also treated to the 'Blue Moon' sound of:

One shoe!

You've only got one shoe!

Let's all laugh at United

Ha ha ha ha ...

Dundee United

Let's all laugh at Dundee
Ha ha ha ha ...

When not laughing at their city neighbours, United fans also sing the anti-Glasgow songs mentioned above.

Dunfermline

Shit fans, no songs.

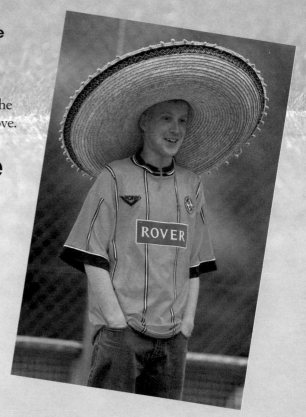

Everton

**Drink, drink, wherever
we may be
He is Duncan
Disorderly
And he will drink a lot
wherever he may be
Cos he is Duncan Disorderly**

A homage to wayward striker Duncan Ferguson to the tune of 'Lord Of
The Dance'.

**It's long, it's thick
It's bigger than his dick
Thompson's nose! Thompson's nose!**

Tune: 'Wem-ber-lee! Wem-ber-lee!'. One of several popular references
to the nose of Liverpool legend and assistant manager Phil Thompson.
Others on the subject include:

It's here, it's there
It's every-f**king-where
Thompson's nose! Thompson's nose!

He's got the whole world in his nose (x4)

Sit down, Pinocchio

To the tune of Verdi's 'La Donna E Mobile'.

You can stick your Michael Owen up your arse (x2)
You can stick your Michael Owen
Stick your Michael Owen
You can stick your Michael Owen up your arse

To the tune of 'She'll Be Coming Round The Mountain'.

Fulham

We're so rich it's unbelievable (*ad infinitum*)

A song not heard at the sleepy Thameside club until the arrival of Harrods owner Mohamed Al-Fayed as chairman.

From Stamford Bridge to Wem-ber-lee
You can stick the blue flag up your arse
Up your arse, up your arse
You can stick the blue flag up your arse

A polite request to their neighbours up the road at Chelsea, mocking the 'Blue Flag Flying High' anthem.

Al Fayed, woo-o-oh
Al Fayed, woo-o-oh
He wants to be a Brit
And QPR are shit

To the tune of 'Volare'. But for every Fulham hymn to their rich Egyptian owner, there at least five responses to be heard from the opposition fans, including:

He's fat, he's round
He's sold your f**king ground
Al-Fayed, Al-Fayed ...

**If your chairman's got a passport, clap your hands
 (x2)
If your chairman's got a passport
Chairman's got a passport
Chairman's got a passport, clap your hands**

A reference to Al-Fayed's unsuccessful application for a British passport.

**Where's your passport (x2)
Where's your passport, Al-Fayed?
Hasn't got one
Never had one
You're a foreigner, Al-Fayed**

Sung to the tune of 'Oh My Darling Clementine'.

**We all agree
Tesco's is better than Harrods**

Gillingham

Two–nil and we f**ked it up

An ironic lament, to the tune of 'Go West', following the Gills' famous second-division play-off final defeat against Man City in 1999. When the teams met again two seasons later, they turned the joke on the City fans:

Two–nil and you all went home

Most anti-Gillingham songs appear to be variations on this theme:

You can't read
You can't write
You wear gold and Nikes
You all come from Gillingham
And you are f**king pikies

Sing when you're palm-reading
You only sing when you're palm-reading

To the tune of 'Guantanamera'.

You can shove your lucky heather up your arse (x2)
You can shove your lucky heather
Shove your lucky heather
You can shove your lucky heather up your arse

To the tune of 'She'll Be Coming Round The Mountain'.

Where's your caravan?
Where's your caravan?

Sung to the tune of 'Where's Your Mama Gone?'

Grimsby Town

Away in a manger

No crib for a bed

The little lord Jesus

He sat up and said

We hate Yorkies and we hate Yorkies (x3)

We are the Yorkie-haters!

A festive message from Humberside. And just in case the Yorkies forgot which county the Ripper hailed from:

There's only one Peter Sutcliffe

One Peter Sutcliffe!

Repeated until bored, then to the tune of 'London Bridge' followed up with:

Yorkshire Ripper is our friend

Is our friend, is our friend

Yorkshire Ripper is our friend

He kills Yorkies!

Short of obvious targets, most opposition fans choose to concentrate on the Grimsby fans' relationship with their favourite supper:

You're shit and you smell of fish (x10)
You're fish and you smell of shit (x10)

To the traditional football tune of 'Go West'.

You only sing when you're fishing
Sing when you're fishing

To the tune of 'Guantanamera'.

Hartlepool United

Apart from the odd blast of Rolf Harris's 'Two Little Boys' and 'We love United' etc, it has been pretty quiet up at Victoria Park in recent years.

Hearts

Jingle bells, jingle bells
Jingle all the way
Oh what fun it is to f**k
The Hibs on New Year's Day, eh!

We're going up, you're going down
We're going to wreck your f**king town
We're going to rape, we're going to pillage
We're going to wreck your f**king village

Ten f**king Hibees sitting on the wall (x2)
And if one f**king Hibee should accidentally fall
There'll be nine f**king Hibees sitting on the wall

Etc. To the tune of 'Ten Green Bottles'.

And now, the end is near
We've followed Hearts from Perth to Paisley
We've travelled far, by bus and car
And other times we've gone by railway
We've been to Aberdeen
We hate the Hibs, they make us spew up
So make a noise, you Gorgie boys
We're going to Europe

To see HMFC
We'll even dig the channel tunnel
When we're afloat on some big boat
We'll tie our scarves around the funnel
We have no cares for other players
Like Rossi, Boniek or Tardelli
When we're overseas, the Hibs will be in Portobelly

To the tune of 'My Way'.

Hibernian

Who do you think you are kidding, Craig Levein
If you think you're number one
We are the boys from the Leith San Siro
We are the boys who have fucked you seven zero

To the *Dad's Army* theme tune. (Levein being the Hearts manager; also sung to his predecessor Jim Jefferies.)

You rake through your buckets for something to eat
You find a dead rat and you call it fresh meat
In your Gorgie slums!

Gorgie being an Edinburgh district and home to Hearts' Tynecastle ground.

Huddersfield Town

Those were the days, my friend
We thought they'd never end
We won the League three times in a row
We won the FA Cup
And then we f**ked it up
We are the Town, oh yes we are the Town

Hull City

He came from Rochdale with a lack of knowledge

He studied management at Bradford College

That's where I ... caught his eye

He told me that he was a manager

I said: In that case you'd better come

   and manage us

He said: Fine

And then, in three seasons' time

He said: I want to take you to the Vauxhall

   Conference

I want to do whatever Halifax do

I want to sign lots of shitty players

I want to watch this club slide out of view

And hoof and hoof and hoof

Because ...

There's nothing left to do

A witty rendition of Pulp's 'Common People' for a former manager.

Have you ever seen a Tiger f**k a fish (x2)

Have you ever seen a Tiger

Ever seen a Tiger

Have you ever seen a Tiger f**k a fish

Tigers fans greeting their friends from Grimsby …

Hey-ey, Brabin

I wanna know-oh-oh

Why you're so crap

Is it cakes, is it chips, is it pies

That make you fat?

To the tune of 'Hey Baby', a cheery welcome for burly midfielder Gary Brabin when he returned with Torquay United.

Visitors to Hull have often struggled for inspiration when it comes to taunting their hosts, but there is always the old favourite:

You can shove your f**king ferries up your arse (x2)
You can shove your f**ing ferries
Shove your f**king ferries
You can shove your f**king ferries up your arse

Tune: 'She'll Be Coming Round The Mountain'.

If desperate, and you come from London and are positively spoilt for river crossings, there is always the Humber's lack of bridges to take a swipe at:

One bridge
You've only got one bridge

Ipswich Town

Finidi Wo-o-o-oh (x2)
He comes from Africa
He drives a big tractor

To the tune of 'Volare', sung by the Tractor boys in praise of Nigerian striker Finidi George.

Oi can't read and Oi can't write
But that don't really ma-er
Cos Oi come from Ipswich Town
Oi can drive a tractor
Oi can plough and milk a cow
And drive a great big mower
But the thing that Oi like best
Is being a potato grower
Oo-ar, Oo-ar to be a Suffolk boy

To which the opposition reply with a cheery:

You only sing when you're farming
Sing when you're farming

Kidderminster Harriers

Shit fans, no songs.

Kilmarnock

Shit fans, no songs.

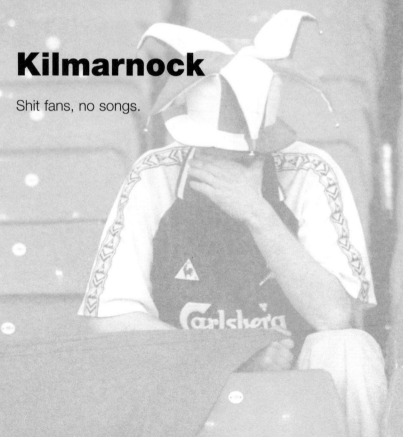

Leeds United

Who do you think you are kidding, Ferguson
If you think you'll win the League
We are the boys who will stop your little game
We are the boys who will put you down to shame
Who do you think you are kidding, Ferguson
If you think old Leeds are done?

To the theme tune of *Dad's Army* and sung for the enjoyment of
Manchester United manager Alex Ferguson.

We've got Dom Matteo
You've got our stereos!

To the tune of 'La Donna E Mobile', sung to Liverpool fans shortly after
Matteo's transfer from one club to the other.

He's here, he's there

He's got no underwear

Lee Bowyer! Lee Bowyer!

Some spontaneous Leeds wit following the midfielder's revelation in court that he sometimes went out in the evening without any pants.

There's a hole in your heart, dear Asa, dear Asa (x10)

Sung to Scotland and Manchester City midfielder Asa Hartford shortly after Leeds rejected the chance to sign him when a medical revealed he did indeed have a hole in his heart.

Chelsea, what's the score?
Chelsea, Chelsea, what's the score?

You had to be there for this one. Chelsea had just thrashed Leeds 5–0 to clinch promotion to the top flight at the end of the 1989 season. Leeds hooligans ripped up the railings and charged the electronic scoreboard repeatedly until every bulb was smashed, then started singing the above. Dark sense of humour, these Northerners.

In recent seasons, however, it has been visiting fans to Elland Road who have had more to sing about as the Yorkshire club, once under former chairman Peter Ridsdale, struggles with titanic financial problems.

Here's to you, Mr Ridsdale

Your team's a joke and you're all broke

God bless you please, Mr Ridsdale

Viduka's fat and Smith's a twat

Oh when Leeds go Nationwide

Oh when Leeds go Nationwide

We'll still be in the Premier

When Leeds go Nationwide

Leicester City

Posh Spice gags all morning
But Beckham's under par
When they do the dirty deed
He wears her Wonderbra!

To the tune of 'My Old Man's A Dustman'. There are lots of verses to this one and different variations from club to club, but they go well beyond the bounds of decency and, sadly, are utterly unprintable.

Always shit on the red side of the Trent
Da da da da da da da da
Forest are total shit
When you think of it
So always shit on
The red side of the Trent

To the tune of Monty Python's 'Always Look On The Bright Side Of Life'.

Oh Dickov is a Scotsman

He wears a Scottish hat

He lives with Brian Deano

In a council flat

He scores 'em with his left foot

He scores 'em with his right

And when we play against Derby

He scores all f**king night

To the tune of 'My Old Man's A Dustman'.

Leyton Orient

Worksop-born defender Gary Bellamy – a tough journeyman pro
with a nice moustache, big muscles, the aura of a nude model and
a PFA representative's card – is the unlikely inspiration behind a
series of witty terrace tunes at Brisbane Road:

Bellamy, Bellamy
Gary Bellamy
He looks so flash
With his Northern Tash
Gary Bellamy ...

Bellamy, Bellamy
Gary Bellamy
He looks so hard
With his union card
Gary Bellamy ...

Bellamy, Bellamy
Gary Bellamy
He looks so hard
Cos he eats his lard
Gary Bellamy ...

Bellamy, Bellamy
Gary Bellamy
He flexed his pecs in
The Joy Of Sex
Gary Bellamy ...

Lincoln City

Mary had a little lamb
Who played in goal a lot
It let the ball go through its legs
So now it's in the pot

Liverpool

We've got a big Pole in our goal (x4)

To the tune of 'He's Got The Whole World In His Hands'. A homage to towering Polish goalkeeper Jerzy Dudek.

One–nil down
Two–one up
Michael Owen won the cup
A world-class Paddy pass gave the lad the ball
Poor old Arsenal won f**k all

Tune: 'Nick Nack Paddy Whack'. Sung after Owen's two late goals, one set up by Danny Murphy (actually an Englishman), gave the Reds a 2–1 win in the 2001 FA Cup final.

You're just too good to be blue

Can't take the ball off you

You've got a heavenly touch

You pass like Souness to Rush

And when were pissed in the bars

We thank the Lord that you're ours

You're just too good to be true

Can't take the ball off you ...

To the tune of 'Can't Take My Eyes Off You'. A homage to Liverpool captain Steven Gerrard.

Livingston

Shit fans, no songs.

Luton Town

Shit fans, no songs.

Macclesfield Town

You can shove your Yorkshire puddings up your
  arse (x2)
You can shove your Yorkshire puddings
Shove your Yorkshire puddings
You can shove your Yorkshire puddings up your
  arse

To the tune of 'She'll Be Coming Round The Mountain'.

Manchester City

Alan Ball, Alan Ball

He's a squeaky ginger bastard

And he's only three foot tall

One for their former manager to the traditional tune of 'Wem-ber-lee! Wem-ber-lee!'.

Who's that twat they call the Keano?

Who's that twat they all adore?

Give him fifty thousand quid

And he'll score for Real Madrid

Now they haven't got the treble any more

To the tune of 'We'll Really Shake 'Em Up When We Win The FA Cup', celebrating Roy Keane's own goal in Manchester United's Champions League defeat against Real Madrid in 2000.

Would you like another Stella, Georgie Best? (x2)
Would you like another Stella
Cos your face is turning yella
Would you like another Stella, Georgie Best?

Would you like another Bud Ice, Georgie Best? (x2)
Would you like another Bud Ice
Cos your face is turning jaundice
Would you like another Bud Ice, Georgie Best?

Would you like another whisky, Georgie Best? (x2)
Would you like another whisky
And fall like Emile Heskey
Would you like another whisky, Georgie Best?

Would you like another Becks, Georgie Best? (x2)
Would you like another Becks
You'll be pissing in your kecks
Would you like another Becks, Georgie Best?

Would you like a Newcy Brown, Georgie Best? (x2)
Would you like a Newcy Brown
You'll soon be six foot down
Would you like a Newcy Brown, Georgie Best?

To the tune of 'She'll Be Coming Round The Mountain'. City fans
showing their sympathy for the chronic alcohol problems of United
legend George Best.

And all the runs that Kinky make are winding
And all the goals that City score are blinding
There are many things that I would like to say to you
But I don't know how
I said maybe
Eike's gonna be the one who saves me
And after all
You're my Alan Ball

To the tune of 'Wonderwall', written by City fan Noel Gallagher. (Kinky is
Georgian midfielder Georghe Kinkladze, Eike is goalkeeper Eike Immel.)

We're the pride of (x2)
We're the pride of Manchester
You're the pride of Singapore

To the tune of 'Bread Of Heaven'. A dig at United's commercial enterprises in the Far East.

Get your hair cut (x2)
Get your hair cut for the lads (x2)

City fans welcome the pony-tailed former England keeper David Seaman to Manchester. Meanwhile, at the other end, the opposition fans are reminding him of his flapping attempt to keep out Ronaldinho's goal, singing 'Let's all do the Seaman' while waving their arms about.

Manchester United

Since City beat United my true love sent to me

European Champions

Eleven years of glory

Ten years in Europe

Nine goals past Ipswich

Eight–one at Forest

Seven past the Cockneys

Six title trophies

Five–nil wins!

Four FA Cups

Treble Ninety-Nine

Two Doubles

And an Eric Cantona

To the tune of 'Twelve Days Of Christmas'.

Twenty-four years just waiting for a chance

To win a major trophy

Give silverware a glance

For twenty-four years we've been living next door
  to City

City, who the f**k are City?

To the tune of Smokie's 'Living Next Door To Alice'.

In the town where I was born

There's a team we all adore

But there's a team that's f**king shite

And they play in blue and white

Singing ...

City's going down like a Russian submarine

A Russian submarine, a Russian submarine

To the tune of 'Yellow Submarine'.

Oh! Keano's f**king magic
He wears a magic hat
And when he saw Old Trafford
He said I fancy that
He didn't sign for Arsenal
Or Blackburn cos they're shite
He signed for Man United
Cos they're fucking dynamite

To the tune of 'My Old Man's A Dustman'. A jaunty tribute to captain Roy Keane.

You are my Solskjaer
My Ole Solskjaer
You make me happy
When skies are grey
And Alan Shearer
Was f**king dearer
So please don't take
My Solskjaer away

To the tune of 'You Are My Sunshine'.

He's fat
He's scouse
He's probably robbed your house
Rooney
Rooney

To the tune of 'Hooray, Hooray, It's A Holi-holiday'.

I met Kevin Keegan
I asked him how City'd do
And do you know what he told me?
Were going back to Division Two

To the tune of 'My Old Man's A Dustman'.

On your Yorkshire farms
You bother the lambs in the long grass
You'd rather shag sheep than a fit normal lass
On your Yorkshire farms

To the tune of 'In Your Northern Slums', this one is generally reserved for United's friends across the Pennines in Leeds.

Dwight Yorke, wherever he may be
He is the king of pornography
And he stuck two fingers up at John Gregory
When he signed for Man U FC

Dwight Yorke, wherever he may be
He is the king of pornography
He left Aston Villa for fear that he'd be shot
So he came to Man United and he won the
   f**king lot

To the tune of 'Lord Of The Dance'.

U-N-I
T-E-D
United are the team for me
With a nick nack paddy whack
Give a dog a bone
Why don't City f**k off home?

Timmy Howard

F**k off

He plays in our net

F**k off

Timmy Howard

F**k off

He's got Tourette's

A curious tribute to their own goalkeeper who indeed does suffer from the neurological disorder Tourette's Syndrome.

Neville Neville, your future's immense

Neville Neville, you play in defence

Neville Neville, like Jacko you're bad

Neville Neville is the name of your dad

Tune: 'Rebel, Rebel' – a homage to the brothers Gary and Phil, whose dad really is called Neville Neville, occasionally prompting the following reaction from opposition fans with a less upbeat view of the Nevilles:

If the Nevilles can play for England so can I (x2)
If the Nevilles can play for England
Nevilles can play for England
If the Nevilles can play for England so can I!

Tune: 'She'll Be Coming Round The Mountain'.

Manchester United were losing at home to Liverpool, whose fans were singing 'Ten men, we've only got ten men' after a sending off, to which the United fans responded with:

'Ten pence, you've only got ten pence!'

Mansfield Town

My garden shed
(My garden shed)
Is bigger than this
(Is bigger than this)
My garden shed is bigger than this
It's got a door and a window
My garden shed is bigger than this

My underpants
(My underpants)
Are bigger than this
(Are bigger than this)
My underpants are bigger than this
There's a fly and some skid marks
My underpants are bigger than this

To the tune of 'When The Saints …'

We're shit and we know we are (x4)

To the tune of 'Go West'.

Middlesbrough

In the town of Sunderland
Lived a man called Peter Reid
And he had a monkey's heed
He peels bananas with his feet
Peter Reid's got a f**king monkey's heed
A f**king monkey's heed
A f**king monkey's heed!

Traditional welcome to the tune of 'Yellow Submarine' for the former Sunderland manager. Popular amongst Newcastle fans too.

One Job on Teesside
There's only one Job on Teesside

A witty pun on the name of Boro striker Joseph Desiree Job.

Steve McClaren came to town
Riding on a pony
Sunderland have got Phil Babb
And we've got Maccarone

We drink X
We drink brown
Were going to wreck your f**king town
With pissed up Boro fans running all around
We'll kill you all outside your ground

To the tune of 'Knick Knack Paddy Whack'.

Millwall

We're the best-behaved supporters in the League
(x2)
We're the best-behaved supporters
Best-behaved supporters
Best-behaved supporters in the League

We're a right bunch of bastards when we lose (x2)
We're a right bunch of bastards
Right bunch of bastards
We're a right bunch of bastards when we lose

Head, shoulders, foot and mouth
Foot and mouth
Head, shoulders, foot and mouth
Foot and mouth

Sung at the height of the foot and mouth crisis at teams from rural areas.

We hate Tuesday
And we hate Tuesday
We are the Tuesday-haters!

In response to Sheffield United fans singing 'We hate Wednesday' etc.

Motherwell

Away the lads
You should've seen us coming
We're only here to drink your beer
And shag your f**king women
All the lads and lassies
Had smiles upon their faces
Walking down the Fir Park Road
To see the Motherwell aces

We are the Well – can't you hear us?
We are the Well – can't you hear us?
Walking along, singing a song
Shitting on the Hibees all the way

Well I've been a muff-diver for many a year
I spent all my money on muff-diving gear
From goggles to flippers and an oxygen tank
If I can't have a muff-dive I'll just have a wank
And it's Moth-er-well
Moth-er-well FC!
They're by far the greatest team the world's ever
seen

To the tune of 'The Wild Rover'.

Newcastle United

He's only a poor little Mackem
His clothes are all tattered and torn
He came for a fight
So we set him alight
And now he won't come back at all

To the tune of 'He's Only A Poor Little Sparrow'. A warm welcome for their friends from Sunderland.

Tell me ma, me ma

I won't be home for tea

We're going to Italy

Tell me ma, me ma

To the tune of 'Que Sera', after Magpies qualified for the Champions League.

Sir John Hall's got the money

Keegan is our boss

They've got Andy Cole

And we don't give a toss

Putting a brave face on sale of crowd favourite Cole to Manchester United. Followed by:

Thank you very much for the seven million

Thank you very, very, very much (x2)

The sum United paid for him.

**Oh the shadow outside is frightening
It's so big it don't let the light in
You see it wherever you go
Thompson's nose! Thompson's nose! Thompson's
nose!**

To the tune of 'Let It Snow', a reference to the Liverpool assistant manager.

We're supposed to be at work! (x4)

To the tune of 'Bread Of Heaven'. Sung in Barcelona after Champions League game was delayed 24 hours by torrential rain.

Northampton Town

Singing aye aye yippy yippy aye

F**k the Posh!

Singing aye aye yippy yippy aye

F**k the Posh!

Singing aye aye yippy

Aye aye yippy

Aye aye yippy yippy aye

F**k the Posh!

One for Peterborough – perhaps more amusing to sing than to listen to…

Norwich City

We shoot burg-lars
I said, we shoot bur-ger-lars

A warning to light-fingered visitors to Carrow Road following the
conviction of Norfolk farmer Tony Martin for doing exactly that.
A number of Martin-related chants have sprung up in recent years,
most of them heard in East Anglia or the East Midlands and including:

Tony Martin is our friend
Is our friend, is our friend
Tony Martin is our friend
He shoots burglars
Shoot the bastards one by one
One by one, one by one
Shoot the bastards one by one
Tony Martin!

To the tune of 'London Bridge'.

He's tall
He's lean
He's a freaky goal machine
Peter Crouch, Peter Crouch

A memorable welcome for the 6 feet 8 striker after his arrival on loan from Aston Villa; variations were also sung at his other clubs QPR and Portsmouth.

Nottingham Forest

In the town where I was born
There's a team we all adore
But there's a team that's f**king shite
And they play in black and white
Singing ...
County's going down like a Russian submarine
A Russian submarine, a Russian submarine

We'd rather bomb Derby than
    Iraq (x2)
We'd rather bomb Derby
Rather bomb Derby
We'd rather bomb Derby than Iraq

To the tune of 'She'll Be Coming Round The Mountain'.

Five–one down and we're still in Europe ...

To the tune of 'You're Going Home In A F**king Ambulance', sung two minutes before the end of Forest's thrashing by Bayern Munich in the UEFA Cup.

Here is one of the more amusing songs directed at Forest fans:

Robin Hood, Robin Hood, riding through the glen
Robin Hood, Robin Hood, with his merry men
Steals from the rich, gives to the poor
[Pause]
Silly c**t, silly c**t, silly c**t

To the tune of 'Robin Hood, Riding Through The Glen'

Notts County

Juve, Juve
It's just like watching Juve (x3)

To the tune of 'Blue Moon'. Forest fans no doubt would find this one especially hilarious, but by and large County have had little to laugh or shout about since they won the FA Cup in 1894. It's all been a bit quiet down at Meadow Lane.

Oldham Athletic

Breeze Hill

It's just like watching Breeze Hill (x3)

To the tune of 'Blue Moon'. Witty parody of 'It's Just Like Watching Brazil' – Breeze Hill is a school near Oldham's Boundary Park ground.

He's French

He's shit

His head's a f**king tit

Barthez, Barthez

A tribute to the shaven-headed former Man United goalkeeper.

Oxford United

Blue moon
You got promoted too soon
Now you're going back down
Conference is coming to town

Sung to the team recently promoted from the Conference.

When the red-red robin comes bob-bob-bobbing
   along
Shoot the bastard, shoot the bastard

One for Oxford's friends down the road at Swindon, aka The Robins, who
might be moved to reply:

You can shove your f**king uni up your arse (x2)
You can shove your f**king uni
Shove your f**king uni
You can shove your f**king uni up your arse

To the tune of 'She'll Be Coming Round The Mountain'. Like Cambridge,
Oxford has also been encouraged to put its boat race in the same place.

Sing when you're rowing

You only sing when your rowing

To the tune of 'Guantanamera'. Visiting fans have been known to follow this one with:

You'll never win the boat race (x10)

Partick Thistle

All I want is a twelve-inch dick

A season ticket for Partick

A Killie fan

To punch and kick

Oh, wouldn't it be lovely

To the tune of 'Wouldn't It Be Lovely'.

I know a lassie
A bonnie, bonnie lassie
She's as tight as the paper on the wall
She's got legs like a spider
I'd love to f**king ride her
Mary from Maryhill

I was just about to hump her
When her tits fell out her jumper
And her knees were banging off the wall
She's got a big fat belly
She is awfully scaly
Mary from Maryhill

If you want to go to heaven when you die
You must wear a Thistle scarf and tie
You must wear a Thistle bonnet
With 'Fuck the Old Firm' on it
If you want to go to heaven when you die
Singing I'm no a Killie I'm a Jag
Singing I'm no a Killie I'm a Jag
Singing I'm no a Killie
Don't be so fucking silly
Singing I'm no a Killie, I'm a Jag
Thank f**k!

To the tune of 'Aye, Aye, Yippee'. (For uninitiated English football followers, The Jags is Partick's nickname, while Killie refers to rivals Kilmarnock.)

Peterborough United

Shit fans, no songs.

Plymouth Argyle

Who the f**k is Edgar Davids? (x3)
Cause we've got Jason Bent! Bent! Bent!

To the tune of 'Glory, Glory, Hallelujah'.

He's big
He's fat
He's had a heart attack
Joe Kinnear, Joe Kinnear

Joe Kinnear's a wanker
He wears a wanker's hat
And when he watches football
He has a heart attack

Some Argyle fans never quite forgave the former Wimbledon and Luton manager for some disparaging comments he made about their team, and were tickled pink when the man collapsed … At least, like some visitors to Home Park, Big Joe didn't start singing:

You can stick your Cornish pasties up your arse
  (x2)
You can stick your Cornish pasties
Stick your Cornish pasties
You can stick your Cornish pasties up your arse

Portsmouth

My old man said
Be a scummer fan
I said f**k off, b***ocks, you're a c**t

Pompey's loyal fans may not be the most original in the country but they have a keen sense of irony, as they showed in their 5–1 FA Cup hammering by Arsenal in 2004 when, to the tune of 'Bread Of Heaven', they sang:

Can we play you (x2)
Can we play you every week? (x2)

Ya-ka-bu-bu-bu

Feed the yak and he will score

To the left, to the right

Feed the yak and he will score

To the tune of Black Lace's 'Agadoo', praise for Pompey's Nigerian striker Aiyegbeni Yakubu.

Port Vale

In the town where I was born

There was a team

We go to see

And we had ten pints of ale

Before we went to see the Vale

We all piss in a red and white hat

A red and white hat

A red and white hat

To the tune of 'Yellow Submarine'. The red and white hat being the property of neighbours Stoke City …

If you can't talk proper, shut your mouths (x2)
If you can't talk proper
Can't talk proper
If you can't talk proper, shut your mouths

To the tune of 'She'll Be Coming Round The Mountain'. Sung to any club from outside London.

We could buy your (x2)
We could buy your whole estate (x2)

To the tune of 'Bread Of Heaven'. Sung to clubs from supposedly deprived areas.

We've got Karl Connolly
You shag your family

Tune: 'La Donna E Mobile'.

Chim chiminee, chim chiminee

Chim chim cheroo

Who needs Sol Campbell when you've got Shittu?

Who's that driving on the pavement?

Who's that crashing through the wall?

He plays in red and white

And he crashes every night

Tony Adams is a donkey after all

Rangers fans react sympathetically to news that the Arsenal defender had crashed while drunk and was later sent to prison for his troubles.

Rangers

We were watching The Bill
What was the score in Seville?

Rangers' fans taunt Celtic after their 2003 UEFA Cup final defeat to Porto. And again and again …

Tell all the Tims you know
That it'll never be three in a row
We were watching The Bill
While you got f**ked in Seville
And it'll never be three in a row

Tell all the Tims you know
The UEFA Cup went to Porto
You never came first
Your beach balls are burst
And you never got three in a row!

To the tune of 'Que Sera'.

A few seasons earlier, Rangers were not slow to pull Celtic up on their humiliating cup defeat to Inverness Caledonian:

When I find myself in times of trouble

Mother Mary comes to me

Singing Glasgow Celtic one, Caley three, Caley three

Celtic one, Caley three

Celtic one, Caley three

Glasgow Celtic one, Caley three, Caley three

Reading

You're Posh, but you're not Royal (x10)

Royals fans taunt Peterborough, aka The Posh, about their lack of class.

You're so quiet
We think you're Aldershot!

He's fat
He's round
He's taking Millwall down
Mark McGhee, Mark McGhee

One for their former manager…

Rochdale

Does your wife? (x2)
Does your wife have woolly hair? (x2)

To the tune of 'Bread Of Heaven' and sung occasionally to Welsh and Yorkshire teams, especially Halifax.

Rotherham United

When I was young I had some sense
I bought a flute for twenty pence
The only tune that I could play was
F**k the Blades and Sheffield Wednesday!

Rushden & Diamonds

Away in the manger, a crib for a bed

The little Lord Jesus sat up and he said

We hate Kettering (x4)

We are the Kettering haters

Not exactly the most original, but it makes an important point and, besides, what else is there to sing in Rushden, apart from:

We're the worst team in the League (x4)

To the tune of 'He's Got The Whole World In His Hands'.

Scunthorpe United

Always shit on the south side of the bridge
La la la la la la la la
Always shit on Laws's f**king head
La la la la la la la la
Lawsy is so shit
When you look at it
He has no talent of his own for sure
So always shit on Laws's f**king head
La la la la la la la la

To the tune of 'Always Look On The Bright Side Of Life' from Monty Python's *Life of Brian*. (Their manager Laws is a Brian too, but maybe not Scunthorpe's Messiah.)

They call them Meggies
They can't afford a telly
They're dirty and they're smelly
The codhead family

Sheffield United

Wednesday!

Whatever will you do?

You're going down to Division Two

And you won't win a cup

And you won't win a shield

And your next derby is Chest-er-field

Wednesday!

Whatever will you do?

You're going down to Division Two

And you can take your trumpet

And take your drum

And go and play with the Barnsley scum

To the tune of 'Lord Of The Dance', a moving farewell to their city rivals with a special word for that annoying Latino-style band.

Dingle bells
Dingle bells
Dingle all the way
O what fun
It is to see
Barnsley go away, hey!

You fill up my senses
Like a gallon of Magnet
Like a packet of Woodbines
Like a good pinch of snuff
Like a night out in Sheffield
Like a greasy chip buttie
Like Sheffield United
Come fill me again!

To the tune of 'Annie's Song'.

Shall we build a (x2)
Shall we build a stand for you? (x2)

To the tune of 'Bread Of Heaven', sung to local rivals Rotherham, whose ground capacity is 11,500.

Sheffield Wednesday

Neil Warnock has a farm
E-I-E-I-O
And on that farm he has some pigs
E-I-E-I-O
With a Woodhouse here and a Devlin there
Here a Quinn, there a Bent
Everywhere a Keith Curle
Neil Warnock has a farm
E-I-E-I-O

Warnock and his Sheffield United players find themselves back in nursery school.

We got one stand bigger than your ground (x2)

We got one stand bigger

One stand bigger

We got one stand bigger than your ground

To the tune of 'She'll Be Coming Round The Mountain', sung to virtually everyone in Division Two.

Gilles de Bilde

Can he fix it?

Gilles de Bilde

Can he f**k!

Words of encouragement for the Belgian striker.

Southampton

Here's to you, Mr Eriksson
Beattie's scoring more than Michael O
Oh, Oh, Oh
God bless you please, Mr Eriksson
Heskey is a joke, and Jeffers cheats
Cheats cheats cheats
And Vassell's crap

To the tune of 'Mrs Robinson', a word in the England manager's ear about striker James Beattie's claim to an England place.

Rosler's Dad's a German
He wears a German hat
He dropped a bomb on Fratton
And we love him just for that

To the tune of 'My Old Man's A Dustman'. Adapted for south coast purposes but originally sung by Man City fans in homage to striker Uwe Rosler, whose father supposedly did drop a bomb on Man United's Old Trafford in the Second World War.

Our Claus in the middle of defence (x2)

To the tune of 'Our House', a tribute to Norwegian defender Claus Lundekvam. It's funny the first time anyway.

On May the first in '76 the boys in yellow and blue
Went up to London Town to show United what to do
And when Stokes's shot hit the back of the net
You should have heard 'em sigh
And when the final whistle went
You should've heard 'em cry
Ha, ha, ha, ha, la, Man United
They're the biggest f**kng wankers in the world

Most songs sung at Southampton seem for some reason to involve tractors and farm animals …

I can't read and I can't write
But that don't really matter
Cos I come from Southampton
I can drive a tractor
I can plough and milk a cow
And drive a great big mower
But the thing that I like best
Is being a strawberry grower
Oo-ar, oo-ar, to be a south-er-nar

Southend United

Oh I do like to be beside the seaside
Oh I do like to be beside the sea
With a bucket and a spade and a f**king hand grenade
Beside the seaside, beside the sea!

Oh Southend pier
Is longer than yours
Oh Southend pier is longer than yours
It's got some shops, and a railway
Oh Southend pier is longer than yours

To the tune of 'When The Saints …'. Size matters for Southend fans when visitors from rival seaside resorts are in town. But the Shrimpers can also laugh at themselves:

Oh the grand old Duke of York
He had 10,000 men
None of them could kick a ball
So he sold them to Southend

Stockport County

He's bald, he's hard
He's known by Scotland Yard
Chrissie Byrne! Chrissie Byrne!

And …

He's always on the run
He's been shot with a gun
Chrissie Byrne! Chrissie Byrne!

Two tributes to hard-nut County star Byrne after he was wounded in a gangland-style shooting. Byrne, who also played for Macclesfield and Sunderland, has helped police with their enquiries on a number of occasions, and was convicted of robbing a chemist in 1999.

Blue Moon
You started singing too soon
You thought that you were win-ning
Then up stepped Tony Din-ning
You started singing too soon

Taunting local rivals Manchester City with a parody of their own anthem after a late winner at Maine Road. (Stockport and Crewe fans insist that they were singing 'Blue Moon' long before City ever got around to claiming it as their own.)

Joe Royle
Whatever you may do
You're going down to Division Two
You won't win a cup
You won't win a shield
Your next derby is Macclesfield

To the tune of 'Lord Of The Dance', rolled out with relish after Royle's Man City were relegated in 1999.

In recent seasons this tasteless ditty, to the tune of 'Bread Of Heaven', has occasionally been heard emanating from the away section at Edgeley Park following the conviction of local doctor Harold Shipman, Britain's worst serial killer:

Did the doctor (x2)

Did the doctor kill your mum? (x2)

Stoke City

We want a tash like
    Ed De Goey, Ed De Goey,
    Ed De Goey
We want a tash like
    Ed De Goey
Super Dutch porn star!

To the tune of 'London Bridge'. A welcome of sorts to the Potteries for the former Chelsea keeper.

Sunderland

The premiership

(The premiership)

Is upside down

(Is upside down)

The premiership is upside down

We're going to Europe with West Brom

The Magpies are going down!

To the tune of 'When The Saints …', sung throughout the 2002/03 season when they finished bottom with a record low points tally of 19.

Niall Quinn's disco pants are the best

They go right from his arse to his chest

They are better than Adam and the Ants

Niall Quinn's disco pants

Surreal praise for the Irishman's clubbing gear …

Wor me lads, all the Toon's a-gannin'
Sheppard and Hall were having a ball
They said in the Sunday papers
Their fans are shite, and not too bright
The lasses have ugly faces
Oh what a terrible stench there is
In the boardroom at St James

Wor me lads, all the Toon's a-gannin'
Gannin' across St James Park
To see the public hanging
Sheppard and Hall, strung up by the balls
With a pair of Keegan's laces
Oh what a beautiful thing to see
The smiles wiped off their fat faces

To the tune of 'Blaydon Races'. Sunderland fans have fun with the Newcastle anthem following the furore surrounding top-ranking officials exposed by an undercover reporter mocking their team's fans and questioning the beauty of the club's female following. Ouch.

There's only one Bobby Robson (x2)
With his pension book and zimmerframe
Bobby Robson's pissed himself again.

Tune: 'Winter Wonderland'.

Swansea City

One–nil to the sheepshaggers (*ad infinitum*)

To the tune of 'Go West'.

**We shag 'em
You eat 'em!**

**I'm dreaming of a white Christmas
Just like the ones I used to know
When the Swans are flying
The Bluebirds are dying
And Lennie Lawrence is wanking in the snow**

Cheery festive greetings for Lennie Lawrence and the boys from Cardiff.

Breaststroke, backstroke, butterfly and crawl
Doggy paddle, belly flop, Cardiff do 'em all
Learn to swim!

A reference to a famous clash of supporters which ended, supposedly, with Cardiff fans fleeing down the pier and hurling themselves into the sea.

Swindon Town

All things bright and beautiful
All creatures great and small
Swindon rule the West Country and Oxford rule f**k all

QPR fans to Swindon:

Going down, going down, going down ...

Swindon fans:

So are we, so are we, so are we ...

Swindon, Swindon, Ra! Ra! Ra!
Oxford, Oxford, Ha! Ha! Ha!
Bristol, Bristol, Ba! Ba! Ba!
Scousers, Scousers, Where's my car?

Torquay United

Bra-zil of the West Country (x2)

To the tune of 'Go West'. Plymouth and Exeter fans are the first to see the humour in this one.

Have you ever (x2)
Have you ever seen a beach? (x2)

To the tune of 'Bread Of Heaven', generally sung to landlocked Midlands clubs.

You dirty northern bastards (*ad infinitum*)

Sung to all teams except Plymouth, even Exeter, to which they might hear the reply:

You can shove your Riviera up your arse (x2)
You can shove your Riviera
Shove your Riviera
You can shove your Riviera up your arse

To the tune of 'She'll Be Coming Round The Mountain'.

Tottenham Hotspur

He's only a poor little Gooner
He stands at the end of the Bank
He watches the Reds
The football he dreads
So he ends up having a wank

I'm only a poor little yiddo
I stand at the back of the Shelf
I go to the bar, to buy a lager
And only buy one for myself.

Tottenham do irony …

We're shit and we're sick of it (*ad infinitum*)

Chim chiminee, chim chiminee

Chim chim cheroo

Jürgen was a German

But now he's a Jew

Ethnic and religious delight at White Hart Lane after the German striker Klinsmann shuns his homeland and collects his North London passport ...

Chim chiminee, chim chiminee

Chim chim cheroo

Nayim was an Arab

But now he's a Jew

Following the arrival of the Moroccan midfielder Nayim in North London ...

The following began to roll off the terraces very shortly after the future Arsenal captain was convicted for drink driving and sent to prison:

Who had all the beers?
Who had all the beers?
Tony Adams, Tony Adams
He had all the beers

To the tune of 'Knees Up Mother Brown'.

Cheer up, Tony Adams
O what can it mean?
To be a pissed-up donkey
In a shit football team

Jingle bells, jingle bells, jingle all the way
Oh what fun it is to see Adams put away, Oh!

Where's your donkey gone?

To the tune of 'Where's Your Mama gone?'

Highbury is a library
Highbury is a library
La la la la ...

To the tune of 'Let's All Do The Conga'.

Who's that team they call the Arsenal?
Who's that team the Greeks adore?
They're the girls in red and white
And they are a load of shite
And *Bloggsy*'s mother is a f**king whore ...

To the tune of 'We'll Really Shake Them Up'.

It's a long way to Seven Sisters
It's a long way to run

Tune: 'It's A Long Way To Tipperary' – the more thoughtful Tottenham fans hand out a travel warning to the visiting fans. No wonder visiting fans have been known to sing:

Sing a song of sixpence
A pocket full of rye
Four and twenty blackbirds baked in a pie
And when the pie was opened the birds began
to sing
We hate Tottenham! And we hate Tottenham!
We are the Tottenham ha-ters!

There's only two Gary Stevens (x2)

Tune: 'Guantanamera'. Sung by Tottenham and Everton during the 1980s when both clubs had a player by that name.

Tranmere Rovers

Don't be mistaken
Don't be misled
We are not Scousers
We're from Birkenhead
You can f**k your cathedral
And your pier head
Cos we are not Scousers
We're from Birkenhead

We hate Scousers
And we hate Scousers
We are the Scouser-haters!

Walsall

We are the pride of the Midlands

The Villa are scum

We hate the Wanderers

The Baggies and Brum

We are the Walsall

We are the best

We are the Saddlers

So f**k all the rest!

Blimey. You'd never guess that Walsall have never made it to the top flight in over 115 years of trying and you might tempted to retort:

Small town in Poland

You're just a small town in Poland

To the tune of 'Guantanamera'.

Watford

Aaa-gaa ... doo-doo-doo
We're the Watford wrecking crew
To the left, to the right
Luton Town are f**king shite

To the tune of Black Lace's 'Agadoo'.

The Luton train came over the hill
The hill, the hill
The Luton train came over the hill
The hill, the hill
The Luton train came over the hill
The brakes failed and they all got killed
Singing, ha, ha, ha, ha, ha, ha

To the tune of 'When Johnny Comes Marching Home Again'.

Vialli woh oh oh

He comes from It-a-ly

He wears Ver-sa-ce

To the tune of 'Volare', Watford fans welcome the arrival of the well-turned-out former Chelsea boss … until they realize he has taken their credit cards and gone on a mad shopping spree in the West End:

Vialli woh oh oh

He came from It-al-y

He spent all our mon-ey

West Bromwich Albion

Taylor is a turnip
He's got a turnip's head
He took the job at Villa
He must have been brain-dead

Do I not like this?
Do I not like that?
Everyone in England knows
He is a f**king twat

To the tune of 'My Old Man's A Dustman' … a touching welcome for the former Villa and Wolves boss.

You're not drinking (x2)
You're not drinking any more (x2)

To the tune of 'Bread Of Heaven' – a witty reminder to visiting fans just before half-time after the Baggies banned alcohol at the Smethwick End stand.

Lip up fatty-o, lip up fatty
Rooney, Rooney ...

A modern Midlands rendition of the Bad Manners classic.

Who's the fattest bastard in Division One?
It's you Ron, Ron, Ron
It's you Ron, Ron

To the tune of 'Da Doo Ron Ron', sung to the well-fed Ron Atkinson when he was in charge of the Midlands club.

West Ham United

World Cup

We won the f**king World Cup (x3)

To the tune of 'Blue Moon'; a reference to the 1966 heroics of Moore, Peters and Hurst.

I remember Wembley

When West Ham beat West Germany.

Martin one and Geoffrey three

And Bobby got the OBE!

Ian wank, wank, wank

A special welcome for Arsenal striker Ian Wright …

Ian Wright, Wright, Wright

A slight change of tune when he signed for the Hammers.

You put your right arm up

The linesman's flag is down

Paolo sticks it in and the scum are one-nil down

They are out of the cup

Cos their goalie just f**ked up

And that's what it's all about

Oh, Fabien Barthez...

To the tune of 'Hokey Cokey'. A summary of events from West Ham's FA Cup win at Old Trafford when Barthez tried to put off Di Canio by claiming he was offside.

My one skin goes over my two skin

My two skin goes over my three

My three skin goes over my foreskin

Oh bring back my foreskin to me!

Bring back, bring back

Oh bring back my foreskin to me!

To the tune of 'My Bonnie Lies Over The Ocean'. Generally reserved for the Hammers' London cousins up the road at Tottenham …

He's small
He's hard
He's got a yellow card
John Moncur, John Moncur!

To the tune of 'Hooray! Hooray! It's a Holi-holiday'.

You can shove your fucking bubbles up your arse
  (x2)
You can shove your fucking bubbles
Shove your fucking bubbles
You can shove your fucking bubbles up your arse

To the tune of 'She'll Be Coming Round The Mountain', for when the Hammers roll out the East End anthem 'I'm Forever Blowing Bubbles'.

Wigan Athletic

We come from Wigan

And we live in mudhuts

Ooh aah, ooh ooh aah

Ooh to be a Wiganer

Don't ask …

A couple of ditties for their Rugby League friends in this close-knit sporting community:

They're stinky and they're smelly

They come from Scholes and Whelley

They haven't got a telly

The Wigan Warriors …

To the *Addams Family* theme tune.

You can stick your f**king rugby up your arse …

To the tune of 'She'll Be Coming Round The Mountain'.

Wimbledon

**Show me the way to Plough Lane
I'm tired and I wanna go home
I had a football ground ten years ago
And I want one of my own
Whenever I may roam to Selhurst Park again
You'll always hear me singing this song
Show me the way to Plough Lane**

This perhaps is only amusing to those who do not follow the Dons …

Since their controversial move from Plough Lane first to Selhurst Park and then to Milton Keynes, Dons have had to endure taunts about their itinerant status …

**No ground, no fans
No ground, no fans**

Tune: 'Big Ben Chimes'.

We are Wombles, we are Wombles
We are Wombles from Plough Lane
We are Wombles, super Wombles
We are Wombles, we drink champagne

We drink champagne, we snort cocaine
We've got ladies over 'ere
You've got shit jobs, you shag your dogs
And your wife is on the game

We drink Campari, we drive Ferraris
We've got ladies over 'ere
You drink John Smiths, you're all blacksmiths
And your toilet's out the rear

We wear Gucci, we wear Armani
We've got cashmere over here
You've got shell suits, Wellington boots
And your fashion's soooooo last year

To the tune of 'Oh My Darling Clementine'. Four verses from a song that is constantly being updated and added to by the real Wimbledon fans. Surely one of the best in recent years.

Wolverhampton Wanderers

Bus stop in Aston
You're just a bus stop in Aston (*ad infinitum*)

To the tune of 'Guantanamera'.

Ri-o
You should have pissed in the cup (x3)

To the tune of 'Blue Moon', Wolves welcome Man United's
Rio Ferdinand to Molineux after the controversy of his failure to take
a random drugs test.

Always shit on a Tesco carrier bag
La la la la la la la la

An oblique reference to the strip of local rivals West Brom, to the tune of
'Always Look On The Bright Side Of Life'.

Wrexham

I'm a bastard

I'm a bastard

I'm a bastard, yes I am

But I'd rather be a bastard

Than a f**king Englishman

To the tune of 'Oh My Darling Clementine'.

We'll burn all your tables
We'll burn all your chairs
We'll burn all your children when sleeping upstairs
In your holiday homes ...

To the tune (if you can call it that) of 'In Your Northern Slums' –
Wrexham boys give the English visitors a toasty warm welcome.

Oh fluffy sheep are wonderful
Oh fluffy sheep are wonderful
They are white, Welsh and fluffy
Oh fluffy sheep are wonderful

To the tune of 'When The Saints ...' A robust defence of the farmland
beast in the face of nasty English taunts about the Welshmen's relationship
with them.

Wycombe Wanderers

We hate Col U
And we hate Col U
We are the Col U ha-ters

… is about as creative and original as it gets at Adams Park.

We've got Craig Faulconbridge (x2)
Why do we sing this song?
He's not Italian.

Tune: Verdi's 'La Donna E Mobile'.

Yeovil Town

Drink up your cider, drink up your cider

For tonight we'll be merry, merry be

We're on our way to Dover

To f**k in the clover

There's plenty more cider in the jar

That, I'm afraid, is the best song to emerge from Yeovil since they joined the League.

York City

Oh the grand old Duke of York
He had eleven men
He marched them up to Old Trafford
And shat on Ferguson
And when there was one there was one
And then there was two there was two
And when they banged the third one in
They knew they'd done Man U!

Celebrating York City's greatest ever day, a stunning 3–0 League Cup win in 1995 over a United side featuring Beckham, Giggs, Phil Neville, Irwin, Pallister, Bruce, Sharpe, McClair and Paul Parker. And just to rub it in:

What's it like to (x2)
What's it like to be outclassed? (x2)

Are you Scarborough (x2)
Are you Scarborough in disguise? (x2)

To the tune of 'Bread Of Heaven'.

You can shove your f**king minster up your arse (x2)
You can shove your f**king minster
Shove your f**king minster
You can shove your f**king minster up your arse

A favourite for visiting fans …

General Chants

You look in the dustbin for something to eat
You find a dead rat and think it's a treat
In your northern slums, in your northern slums!

You piss in the shower
You shit in the bath
You finger your Gran and think it's a laugh
In your northern slums, in your northern slums!

Your dad's in the nick
Your mum's on the game
In your northern slums, in your northern slums!

You look at your dog in a frisky way
You give it a f**k and throw it away
In your northern slums, in your northern slums!

And a variation on the same family theme:

Me brother's in borstal

Me sister's got pox

Me mother's a whore on the Liverpool Docks

Me uncle's a flasher

Me auntie's a slag

The Yorkshire Ripper's me dad!

There's only one *Bryan Bloggs*

One *Bryan Bloggs*

With his packet of sweets

And his cheeky smile

***Bloggsy* is a f**king paedophile**

To the tune of 'Winter Wonderland'. Supply name of choice. Likewise:

Bloggsy, wherever you may be
You are the king of child pornography
He goes in the showers with his little youth team
And while he's in there you should hear them
   scream

To the tune of 'Lord Of The Dance'.

Chim chiminee, chim chiminee
Chim chim cheroo
How is life in Division One treating you?

Works just as well with teams recently relegated to Division Two
and Three.

You're shit and you're nearly Welsh (x2)

And:

You're Welsh and you know you are (x2)

Both sung to border towns like Hereford, Chester and Shrewsbury,
to the tune of 'Go West'.

Who ate all the pies? (x2)
You fat bastard (x2)
You ate all the pies!

And the sausage rolls (x2)
You fat bastard (x2)
And the sausage rolls!

And the pasties too (x2)
You fat bastard (x2)
And the pasties too!

To the tune of 'Knees Up Mother Brown'.

Keeper, keeper, where's your wife?
She's here
She's there
She's every-f**king-where
She's a slag
She's a slag

Does she take it (x2)

Does she take it up the arse? (x2)

To the tune of 'Bread Of Heaven'. A popular one for players with pretty celebrity wives.

Go tut dole, cash Giro

Go tut pub, get plastered

Come home, beat up wife

Cos I'm a Northern bastard

I've got a shed

It's bigger than this

I've got a shed that's bigger than this

It's got a door and a window

I've got a shed that's bigger than this

My rabbit hutch

Is bigger than this

My rabbit hutch is bigger than this

It's got a door and a rabbit

My rabbit hutch is bigger than this

To the tune of 'When The Saints Go Marching In'. Sung by visiting fans to small grounds. And in a similar vein, the old classic:

Shit ground no fans, shit ground no fans

Shit fans no songs, shit fans no songs

Shit fans no pride, shit fans no pride

To the tune of 'Big Ben Chimes'. And while we're about it:

A town full of in-breds!

You're just a town full of in-breds!

To the tune of 'Guantanamera'.

As for that useless ref:

All we want is a decent referee

A decent referee, a decent referee, a decent
  referee

To the tune of 'Yellow Submarine'.

The ref has got a tenner on the game (x2)

The ref has got a tenner (x2)

The ref has got a tenner on the game

To the tune of 'She'll Be Coming Round The Mountain'.

Who's your father? (x2)

Who's your father, referee?

You ain't got one

You're a bastard

You're a bastard, referee

To the tune of 'Oh My Darling Clementine'.

The referee's
Got BSE
The referee's got BSE
He eats beef, beef and more beef
The referee's got BSE

The referee's
Got foot and mouth
The referee's
Got foot and mouth etc

To the tune of 'When The Saints Go Marching In'.

We know where you live (x2)
You fat bastard (x2)
We know where you live!

To the tune of 'Knees Up Mother Brown'.

You're not fit to (x2)
You're not fit to ref non-League (x2)

You're not fit to (x2)
You're not fit to wipe my arse (x2)

To the tune of 'Bread Of Heaven'.

Are you Stevie (x2)
Are you Stevie Wonder in disguise? (x2)

To the tune of 'Bread Of Heaven'.

Sign on, sign on
With a pen
In your hand
You'll never work again
Sign on, sign on

To the tune of 'You'll Never Walk Alone'. Sung mainly at Everton and Liverpool fans, and often followed by:

You've got our stereos
TVs and videos ...

To the tune of Verdi's 'La Donna E Mobile'.

Thank you very much for paying our Giros
Thank you very much, thank you very very very
much
Thank you very much for paying our Giros
Thank you very very very much

What the Liverpool and Everton fans like to sing in reply.

**They had to grease the turnstile just to get the
bastard in (x3)**
For he's a big fat bastard

To the tune of 'Mine Eyes Have Seen The Glory'. Sung on sight of a fat
spectator.

Bryan Bloggs is a virgin (*supply name of player or manager*)
He's never used his dick
He wanks in the shower
And sleeps in his own sick
He throws up to the left
He throws up to the right
And he couldn't pull a bird
If he tried all f**king night

To the tune of 'My Old Man's A Dustman'.

Cheerio, cheerio, cheerio (x3)
Cheerio, cheerio

To the tune of 'Here We Go'.

Who's that man with the helmet on?
Dixon, Dixon
Who's that man with the helmet on?
Dixon of Dock Green
On the beat all day, on the wife all night
Who's that man with the helmet on?
Dixon of Dock Green

Sung on the appearance of an officer of the constabulary.

The Bill!
It's just like watching The Bill

To the tune of 'Blue Moon'. Known to be sung when there is
a large police presence at a match. As is:

Shit job, no friends
Shit job, no friends

To the tune of 'Big Ben Chimes'.

When I was just a little boy
I asked my mother – what will I be?
Will I be Chelsea? Will I be Spurs?
Here's what she said to me:
Wash your mouth out, son
Go get your father's gun
And shoot some Tottenham scum
It's the Reds for you.

To the tune of 'Que Sera'. A classic sung by most clubs, changing names of local rivals where appropriate. Likewise with another traditional terrace song:

Tottenham Hotspur football club went to see
  the Pope (x3)
And this is what he said:
Who the f**k are Tottenham Hotspur? (x3)
The Reds go marching on, on, on!

To the tune of 'Mine Eyes Have Seen The Glory'.

**Bryan Bloggs is illegitimate (replace with name of
least favourite player)**
He ain't got no birth certificate
He's got Aids and can't get rid of it
**He's a Belgian bastard! (replace with appropriate
country/region)**

Tune: virtually none.

In church
It's just like being in church

To the tune of 'Blue Moon'. One for especially quiet home supporters.

You've got the ugliest stewards in the land (x3)

To the tune of 'The Whole World In Our Hands'.

Sit down you twat (x3)
Sit down
Sit down you twat (x3)
Sit down

To the tune of 'Auld Lang Syne'. Sung at spectators arriving late or leaving early; or when opposition fans rise from their seats when one of their players is through on goal.

We'll be running round Wembley with our willies
  hanging out (x2)
We'll be running round Wembley, running round
  Wembley
Running round Wembley with our willies hanging out
Singing I've got a bigger one than you (x2)
I've got a bigger, I've got a bigger, I've got a bigger
  one than you

To the tune of 'She'll Be Coming Round The Mountain'.

The following are all traditionally sung to the tune of 'Bread Of Heaven':

Does the Social (x2)
Does the Social know you're here? (x2)

What's it like (x2)
What's it like to be a twat? (x2)

Shall we sing a (x2)
Shall we sing a song for you? (x2)

You're not fit (x2)
You're not fit to shag my mum (x2)

Does your mother (x2)
Does your mother know your dad? (x2)

You're not famous (x2)
You're not famous any more (x2)

Sung to big clubs fallen on relatively hard times. In recent years this has been sung mainly at Liverpool and Nottingham Forest.

Does your mother (x2)
Does your mother know you're here? (x2)

Sung a lot to Michael Owen when he emerged as a teenager, but all baby-faced youngsters get the same treatment. See also:

Back to school on Monday!
Back to school on Monday!

Does your mother (x2)
Does your mother know you're queer? (x2)

We can see you (x2)
We can see you sneaking out! (x2)